Francis Frith's
Yorkshire
Coastal Memories

Photographic Memories

Francis Frith's
Yorkshire
Coastal Memories

Maureen Anderson

First published in the United Kingdom in 2002 by
Frith Book Company Ltd

Paperback Edition 2002
ISBN 1-85937-506-5

British Library Cataloguing in Publication Data

Francis Frith's Yorkshire Coastal Memories

Frith Book Company Ltd
Frith's Barn, Teffont,
Salisbury, Wiltshire SP3 5QP
Tel: +44 (0) 1722 716 376
Email: info@francisfrith.co.uk
www.francisfrith.co.uk

Printed and bound in Great Britain

Front Cover: Staithes, The Beach c1955 S176032

AS WITH ANY HISTORICAL DATABASE THE FRITH ARCHIVE IS CONSTANTLY BEING CORRECTED AND IMPROVED
AND THE PUBLISHERS WOULD WELCOME INFORMATION ON OMISSIONS OR INACCURACIES

Contents

Francis Frith: *Victorian Pioneer*

FRANCIS FRITH, Victorian founder of the world-famous photographic archive, was a complex and multi-talented man. A devout Quaker and a highly successful Victorian businessman, he was both philosophic by nature and pioneering in outlook.

By 1855 Francis Frith had already established a wholesale grocery business in Liverpool, and sold it for the astonishing sum of £200,000, which is the equivalent today of over £15,000,000. Now a multi-millionaire, he was able to indulge his passion for travel. As a child he had pored over travel books written by early explorers, and his fancy and imagination had been stirred by family holidays to the sublime mountain regions of Wales and Scotland. 'What a land of spirit-stirring and enriching scenes and places!' he had written. He was to return to these scenes of grandeur in later years to 'recapture the thousands of vivid and tender memories', but with a different purpose. Now in his thirties, and captivated by the new science of photography, Frith set out on a series of pioneering journeys to the Nile regions that occupied him from 1856 until 1860.

Intrigue and Adventure

He took with him on his travels a specially-designed wicker carriage that acted as both dark-room and sleeping chamber. These far-flung journeys were packed with intrigue and adventure. In his life story, written when he was sixty-three, Frith tells of being held captive by bandits, and of fighting 'an awful midnight battle to the very point of surrender with a deadly pack of hungry, wild dogs'. Sporting flowing Arab costume, Frith arrived at Akaba by camel seventy years before Lawrence, where he encountered 'desert princes and rival sheikhs, blazing with jewel-hilted swords'.

During these extraordinary adventures he was assiduously exploring the desert regions bordering the Nile and patiently recording the antiquities and peoples with his camera. He was the first photographer to venture beyond the sixth cataract. Africa was still the mysterious 'Dark Continent', and Stanley and Livingstone's historic meeting was a decade into the future. The conditions for picture taking confound belief. He laboured for hours in his wicker dark-room in the sweltering heat of the desert, while the volatile chemicals fizzed dangerously in their trays. Often he was forced to work in remote tombs and caves where conditions were cooler. Back in London he exhibited his photographs and was 'rapturously cheered' by members of the Royal Society. His reputation as a photographer was made overnight. An eminent modern historian has likened their impact on the population of the time to that on our own generation of the first photographs taken on the surface of the moon.

Venture of a Life-Time

Characteristically, Frith quickly spotted the opportunity to create a new business as a specialist publisher of photographs. He lived in an era of immense and sometimes violent change. For the poor in the early part of Victoria's reign work was a drudge and the hours long, and people had precious little free time to enjoy themselves. Most had no transport other than a cart or gig at their disposal, and had not travelled far beyond the boundaries of their own town or village. However,

by the 1870s, the railways had threaded their way across the country, and Bank Holidays and half-day Saturdays had been made obligatory by Act of Parliament. All of a sudden the ordinary working man and his family were able to enjoy days out and see a little more of the world.

With characteristic business acumen, Francis Frith foresaw that these new tourists would enjoy having souvenirs to commemorate their days out. In 1860 he married Mary Ann Rosling and set out with the intention of photographing every city, town and village in Britain. For the next thirty years he travelled the country by train and by pony and trap, producing fine photographs of seaside resorts and beauty spots that were keenly bought by millions of Victorians. These prints were painstakingly pasted into family albums and pored over during the dark nights of winter, rekindling precious memories of summer excursions.

The Rise of Frith & Co

Frith's studio was soon supplying retail shops all over the country. To meet the demand he gathered about him a small team of photographers, and published the work of independent artist-photographers of the calibre of Roger Fenton and Francis Bedford. In order to gain some understanding of the scale of Frith's business one only has to look at the catalogue issued by Frith & Co in 1886: it runs to some 670 pages, listing not only many thousands of views of the British Isles but also many photographs of most European countries, and China, Japan, the USA and Canada — note the sample page shown above from the hand-written *Frith & Co* ledgers detailing pictures taken. By 1890 Frith had created the greatest specialist photographic publishing company in the world,

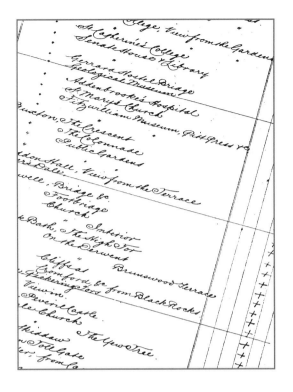

Frith's death, a new card measuring 5.5 x 3.5 inches became the standard format, but it was not until 1902 that the divided back came into being, with address and message on one face and a full-size illustration on the other. *Frith & Co* were in the vanguard of postcard development, and Frith's sons Eustace and Cyril continued their father's monumental task, expanding the number of views offered to the public and recording more and more places in Britain, as the coasts and countryside were opened up to mass travel.

Francis Frith died in 1898 at his villa in Cannes, his great project still growing. The archive he created continued in business for another seventy years. By 1970 it contained over a third of a million pictures of 7,000 cities, towns and villages. The massive photographic record Frith has left to us stands as a living monument to a special and very remarkable man.

with over 2,000 outlets – more than the combined number that Boots and WH Smith have today! The picture on the right shows the *Frith & Co* display board at Ingleton in the Yorkshire Dales. Beautifully constructed with mahogany frame and gilt inserts, it could display up to a dozen local scenes.

Postcard Bonanza

The ever-popular holiday postcard we know today took many years to develop. In 1870 the Post Office issued the first plain cards, with a pre-printed stamp on one face. In 1894 they allowed other publishers' cards to be sent through the mail with an attached adhesive halfpenny stamp. Demand grew rapidly, and in 1895 a new size of postcard was permitted called the court card, but there was little room for illustration. In 1899, a year after

Frith's Archive: *A Unique Legacy*

FRANCIS FRITH'S legacy to us today is of immense significance and value, for the magnificent archive of evocative photographs he created provides a unique record of change in 7,000 cities, towns and villages throughout Britain over a century and more. Frith and his fellow studio photographers revisited locations many times down the years to update their views, compiling for us an enthralling and colourful pageant of British life and character.

We tend to think of Frith's sepia views of Britain as nostalgic, for most of us use them to conjure up memories of places in our own lives with which we have family associations. It often makes us forget that to Francis Frith they were records of daily life as it was actually being lived in the cities, towns and villages of his day. The Victorian age was one of great and often bewildering change for ordinary people, and though the pictures evoke an impression of slower times, life was as busy and hectic as it is today.

We are fortunate that Frith was a photographer of the people, dedicated to recording the minutiae of everyday life. For it is this sheer wealth of visual data, the painstaking chronicle of changes in dress, transport, street layouts, buildings, housing, engineering and landscape that captivates us so much today. His remarkable images offer us a powerful link with the past and with the lives of our ancestors.

Today's Technology

Computers have now made it possible for Frith's many thousands of images to be accessed almost instantly. In the Frith archive today, each photograph is carefully 'digitised' then stored on a CD Rom. Frith archivists can locate a single photograph amongst thousands within seconds. Views can be catalogued and sorted under a variety of categories of place and content to the immediate benefit of researchers.

Inexpensive reference prints can be created for them at the touch of a mouse button, and a wide range of books and other printed materials assembled and published for a wider, more general readership - in the next twelve months over a hundred Frith local history titles will be published! The day-to-day workings of the archive are very different from how they were in Francis Frith's time: imagine the herculean task of sorting through eleven tons of glass negatives as Frith had to do to locate a particular sequence of pictures! Yet

See Frith at www.francisfrith.co.uk

the archive still prides itself on maintaining the same high standards of excellence laid down by Francis Frith, including the painstaking cataloguing and indexing of every view.

It is curious to reflect on how the internet now allows researchers in America and elsewhere greater instant access to the archive than Frith himself ever enjoyed. Many thousands of individual views can be called up on screen within seconds on one of the Frith internet sites, enabling people living continents away to revisit the streets of their ancestral home town, or view places in Britain where they have enjoyed holidays. Many overseas researchers welcome the chance to view special theme selections, such as transport, sports, costume and ancient monuments.

We are certain that Francis Frith would have heartily approved of these modern developments in imaging techniques, for he himself was always working at the very limits of Victorian photographic technology.

The Value of the Archive Today

Because of the benefits brought by the computer, Frith's images are increasingly studied by social historians, by researchers into genealogy and ancestory, by architects, town planners, and by teachers and schoolchildren involved in local history projects.

In addition, the archive offers every one of us an opportunity to examine the places where we and our families have lived and worked down the years. Highly successful in Frith's own era, the archive is now, a century and more on, entering a new phase of popularity.

The Past in Tune with the Future

Historians consider the Francis Frith Collection to be of prime national importance. It is the only archive of its kind remaining in private ownership and has been valued at a million pounds. However, this figure is now rapidly increasing as digital technology enables more and more people around the world to enjoy its benefits.

Francis Frith's archive is now housed in an historic timber barn in the beautiful village of Teffont in Wiltshire. Its founder would not recognize the archive office as it is today. In place of the many thousands of dusty boxes containing glass plate negatives and an all-pervading odour of photographic chemicals, there are now ranks of computer screens. He would be amazed to watch his images travelling round the world at unimaginable speeds through network and internet lines.

The archive's future is both bright and exciting. Francis Frith, with his unshakeable belief in making photographs available to the greatest number of people, would undoubtedly approve of what is being done today with his lifetime's work. His photographs, depicting our shared past, are now bringing pleasure and enlightenment to millions around the world a century and more after his death.

Yorkshire Coastal Memories
An Introduction

Note: many of the towns and villages included in this book on the Yorkshire coast are now part of Humberside. Because this is a book about Yorkshire as it was during the 1950s and 1960s, it was felt appropriate that these locations should be included and written about. Rugged terrain, rocky cliffs, peaceful woodland, flat, seemingly endless beaches, ever-changing moods of the sea, a diversity of wildlife, timeless beauty and much more: all of these have attracted the visitor to the Yorkshire coast for hundreds of years.

Almost without exception, in every town and village, Roman, Bronze Age and Iron Age remains have been unearthed. The banks of the rivers and the shores of the sea were the ideal places for early settlements to be established.

Everything on the coast was not always peaceful. There have been battles against invasion throughout the centuries; excise men have chased smugglers both on land and at sea; and thousands of lives have been lost owing to shipwrecks. The small cobles and the masted sailing vessels did not have the power to withstand the ferocity of the severe gales and storms that often sweep in from the north. If a vessel was blown too close to shore, it could be dashed to pieces either on the rocks that were hidden beneath

the waves or on the huge, almost perpendicular cliffs, some over 400 feet high, that appear to grow straight out of the sea. At low tide the rocky outcrops, stretching out from the land, become visible (they are known as 'scars' - the word derives from 'sker', a Norse word for rock).

The lifeboats were, and still are, manned voluntarily. These brave men would risk their lives to save others, but all too often the launching of the lifeboat would be in vain; the angry, boiling sea would not let them near enough to a stricken vessel to perform a rescue. The villagers that witnessed these tragedies must have felt heartsick and helpless. The bodies of the seafarers would often wash up on the beaches, and would be buried in the local graveyard. Sometimes the lifeboat crew themselves would perish. To aid seafarers, many lighthouses were erected in the 19th century; quite a few of them remain. Battered by wind for a hundred years or more, many have stood the test of time, showing that Victorian workmanship was strong and durable even without the tools and technology that we have today.

During Queen Victoria's reign, the working classes suddenly found themselves with more leisure time. With the coming of the railways, they also had a cheap and easy form of transport. What better place to get away from the smog and drudgery of their cramped workplaces and towns than the seaside? Thus the places that had previously been fishing villages were suddenly catering not just for the middle and upper classes, but for visitors in the thousands. Small fishermen's cottages were knocked down, and large, elegant guesthouses and hotels were built in their place. Along the sea fronts, billiard rooms, souvenir shops, cafés and penny arcades were opened; stalls were placed along the beaches, selling tea and coffee and newspapers. Swings, roundabouts, and donkeys appeared to keep the children amused. Palmists and photographers set up their tents. Punch and Judy argued and bickered to the delight of the young and old alike. Later, ferris wheels and helter-skelters made an appearance.

Nannies and mothers would wheel their perambulators with their other small charges in tow, and then perhaps rest or have a gossip in the well-manicured gardens and parks that were laid out in the popular resorts. Bandstands were a popular venue in most of the resorts, and the entertainment would include minstrels, pierrots and brass bands. A man would often go around rattling a moneybox and selling programmes at a penny a sheet. Pleasure piers and promenades were built for the gentlemen to parade and the ladies to show off the latest fashions as they strolled up and down twirling their parasols.

Kiosks at the entrance to the piers would sell buckets and spades, souvenirs and trinkets; sometimes a kiosk would be used as a tollbooth, if there were a charge to walk on the pier. The piers often had a pavilion where dancing and

entertainments took place. Many of the piers have now disappeared, sad to say. Some have been destroyed by fire, some by ships ramming into them during storms, and others by the continuous battering effects of the wind and the sea.

One of the remaining pleasure piers is at Cleethorpes, which was built in 1873 and the pavilion in 1888. In 1903 the pavilion was destroyed by fire, and in 1905 shops, a café and a new pavilion were erected. The pavilion has changed hands and fortunes over the years, but both the pier and pavilion have managed to survive. Another surviving pier is at Saltburn. When it opened in 1869, it was over a quarter of a mile in length until a ship, the 'Ovenberg', rammed into it and reduced its length to about 600 feet. The pier has recently undergone a £2,000,000 restoration; let us hope that this will preserve it for another century or more.

Bathing machines were invented in the 18th century, and Scarborough was the first resort on the north-east coast to introduce them to its beach. These contraptions, looking a little like gypsy caravans, were pulled manually or by horse a little way out into the bay. They were used to protect the modesty of the bathers, for decorum was very much an issue with the strait-laced Victorians. The men's machines would be kept a little way apart from the ones used by the women and children. There was often a 'dipper', or bathing machine attendant, who would assist the ladies and the smaller children in and out of the water.

The machines gave way to dressing tents in the early years of the 20th century. The tents were sometimes triangular-shaped, rather like a flatter version of an Indian tepee - this shape was often used by girl guides and boy scouts. Most of the tents, however, were oblong and box-shaped, made in plain or striped material, and often gaily-coloured. Deck chairs were hired out in the hundreds; dotted all over the beaches, the combination of tents and chairs would make it look as though there was a military exercise being carried out.

Beach fashions were quite startling and cumbersome in the 19th century. Long skirts with an abundance of petticoats, short boots, and large hats, often tied on with a sheer scarf to keep it from being blown away by the sea breezes, were worn by the ladies. Towards the end of the century, the skirts became shorter, the hats became sunbonnets, and the boots became sandals. The men were just as fashion-conscious: they wore heavy dark suits with waistcoats, and top hats or bowlers. These eventually gave way to lighter-weight casual suits worn with trilbys or straw boaters.

Comfortable accommodation was an essential part of the Victorian holiday, just as it is now. Many of the locals obtained work in the hotels and lodging houses as waiters, coachmen, stable hands, chambermaids, laundresses and cooks. In the better hotels and lodgings, the rooms would be large, with open fires and clean linen daily. The food

would be varied and plentiful, usually consisting of local produce, especially fish and shellfish. Salt water bathing was considered to be a cure for minor ailments and very healthy for body and mind: it was not only in the sea in which people indulged in this pleasure, for there were also hot and cold salt water bath houses. Spa or 'spaw' water was also considered curative and healthful. The towns and villages, such as Scarborough, where this natural spring water had been discovered had been attracting visitors for many years before the Victorian era.

The smaller villages along the cliffs, although not so busy as the resorts which had large expanses of sandy beaches, still had their share of visitors. The Victorians loved to explore, so places such as Staithes, Runswick and Robin Hood's Bay must have appealed to their sense of adventure. They liked nothing better than to poke around the narrow lanes that wove in and out between the jumble of little houses, looking into gardens full of lobster pots, old bits of fishing net and other relics of the locals' livelihood. As an added bonus, there were the stories of hidden contraband, smugglers and excise men to feed their imagination. Other, smaller secluded coves, sheltered by the tall cliffs, were ideal for a picnic blanket to be laid out; while the adults sat drinking tea and eating sandwiches, the children could explore the rock pools, in which they would find all sorts of strange marine life.

Over the ages, famous people have left their marks on the towns and villages. Captain James Cook was in Staithes for a time before going to Whitby. His first experience as a sailor was in 1747, when he left from Whitby on the 'Freelove', a coal carrier. Later, the ships that were to give him fame as an explorer were built in the docks here. Anne Bronte loved Scarborough, and visited the town many times. Upon her death from tuberculosis, she was buried in St Mary's churchyard; her grave is visited by hundreds of people every year. Whitby also found fame with the writing of Bram Stoker's 'Dracula' in 1897. Much of the book was centred round the old cobbled streets and Gothic buildings of the old part of the town. More recently, in 1936, the world-famous aviator, Amy Johnson, opened Sewerby Hall, near Bridlington. The hall was built in the early 18th century. Now a museum, it holds many artifacts and mementos relating to Amy's life and career.

The Cleveland Way from Filey to Saltburn, part of the Heritage Coast, is a path that follows ever-changing, spectacular scenery, much of it now protected as a nature reserve. The route would once have echoed to the sound of fishermen shouting to one another as they launched their cobles from the bays below the cliffs, and to the clip-clop of horse's hooves as our ancestors went about their business in carriages or carts. Now walkers, cyclists and artists use the trails for relaxation, or to capture the views on camera and canvas.

Immingham, The 'Tor Anglia' c1965 141034
Administered under one port authority with Grimsby, which is six miles away, this is a deep-water port specialising in bulk mineral cargoes. The large ferry and its sister ship the 'Tor Hollandia' operated between Immingham, Amsterdam and Gothenburg.

Around the Humber

The boundaries of the counties of England are forever changing, which can make it very confusing for the residents. Up as far as Flamborough, the area once came under Humberside. The Humber, the wide river that is formed by the confluence of the Ouse, into which many of Yorkshire's rivers flow, separates Yorkshire from Lincolnshire. The word Humber is Celtic, and means 'good water' or 'good well'. The Humber Bridge crosses the river on the outskirts of Hull; work began on the bridge in 1972, and it was completed in 1981.

Because rivers provided everything that was needed for survival, early Man would form settlements along the banks; the Humber was no exception. It gave a clear view of would-be invaders, close access to the sea for fishing and for the transportation of goods, so it was inevitable that as time went on the small settlements would become towns.

The Spurn lighthouse is situated on the south-eastern tip of the Holderness plain on a narrow, sandy promontory, known as the spit, on the north bank of the Humber estuary - it is one of the largest river estuaries in England. The spit has been used for centuries as a strategic point for lighthouses and beacons to guide shipping. It is about 5 km long, and because it is made up of sand and silt, it is unstable. Thus it only keeps its shape for a relatively short time. Every 250 years or so, it is reconstructed at a slightly different location to the west of its present position. History tells us that there have been at least five Spurn Points. The area ▶

is a haven for naturalists: it is teeming with bird life, and it also has many plants that are unique to this strange part of England. It is now a National Nature Reserve.

Cleethorpes began as a resort in 1863, when a single railway line was opened from Grimsby, although earlier in 1844 it had already been predicted that the town would become busy thanks to the network of the new railways. In 1884 a multi-track railway came into being, and the town became a bustling resort. In the early 19th century Cleethorpes oysters became famous, and were shipped by rail to places such as Leeds and Sheffield. However, in 1903 there was a typhoid epidemic in Sheffield. The sewage outfall at Cleethorpes was blamed, and the oyster industry collapsed. The pier was built in the early 1880s, and in 1902 improvements to the sea defences and the foreshore were carried out on land reclaimed beyond Brighton slipway. To the present day, Cleethorpes remains a popular tourist spot.

A legend (or fact?) relates that a poor Lincolnshire farmer named Grim gave Grimsby its name. There are different versions of the legend. One is that Grim rescued a young Danish prince ▶

◀ **Grimsby**
The Docks 1893 33272
The trawlers still go from here daily, but only a very few since the decline of the fishing industry. A multi-million pound investment in a new fish market in the 1990s has made the town the UK centre for handling fish, although the Grimsby trawlers now only catch a small portion of the fish.

Grimsby
The Town Hall 1890
26726
This was the fourth town hall to be built on the site. The Prince Consort laid the foundation stone for the present building in 1849. In 1854 Queen Victoria officially opened the hall, and Victoria Street was named in honour of the occasion.

▼ Grimsby
Alexandra Dock 1904 51829
As the trawlers became bigger and the catches larger, a second fish dock was opened in 1886. This called for other industries to become involved, and the Grimsby Coal and Tanning Company opened. One vessel seems to be carrying coal. A tall ship in all its splendour can be seen at the far end of the dock.

◄ Grimsby
The Fish Docks c1955
G60019
The dock tower built in 1852 rises in the background. It was 309 feet high, and it contained a clever hydraulic system for working the dock gates. After 40 years' service it became redundant, but it still stands as a symbol of past glories. Three of the vessels moored here are all named with the prefix 'Lady'.

when he was cast out in a boat after his father was murdered. Grim brought the boy up as his own. Eventually the prince returned to his homeland and won back his kingdom, and then rewarded Grim handsomely; Grim used the money to found a town.

Grimsby became the most important fishing port in the country when the railway linked the town with London in 1856. A large fish dock was built; it contained a floating pontoon which rose and fell with the tide. Throughout most of the 19th century, wooden fishing smacks were used, but there was a limit on the distance these could travel in the search for fish. In 1858, a building was erected to store ice. At first it was collected from

**Grimsby
The Fish Pontoon
1906** 55748
Here all is ready for one of the fish auctions that were held daily. Buyers came from all over the country. Much of the fish would end up on the tables of the London hotels. By this time, the large steam-powered boats had taken over from the smacks and trawlers, waters were over-fished, and it was becoming more and more difficult to make a living with the smaller boats.

ponds, but there was never enough, so the ice was brought from Norway. Eventually an ice factory was built. As time went on the trawlers began using steam power and became bigger. This meant that the trawlers could sail great distances and freeze the fish, so they could trawl for larger catches and stay at sea longer. Fishing declined in the 20th century, but Grimsby still remains one of the most important fish docks in Europe. Another claim to fame is that frozen peas and fish fingers were invented here. Nearby Immingham is linked to Grimsby by the Port Authority; it is also an important port on the river, handling mineral cargoes in bulk.

◄ **Grimsby**
The Bull Ring c1965
G60057
The name 'Bull Ring' is quite common in England: it relates to the site of the cruel sport of bull and bear baiting. A number of dogs would be put in an arena, usually with a bull, as bears were rare. All the animals would usually end up with severe injuries, and at the end of the spectacle, the bull would be killed.

◀ **Grimsby**
The Fish Pontoon
1906 55749
Posing for the camera behind the rows of whiting, cod, halibut, plaice, turbot, sole and haddock are the fish dock workers and the prospective fish buyers. The two rather large, white-coated men are enjoying a puff on their pipes before their job of sorting the fish for the buyer starts.

▼ **Grimsby**
The Old Market Place
c1965 G60082
This area was changed dramatically a few years before the photographs were taken. The large building in the centre of the view is the Pestle and Mortar, a 19th-century inn. The mock Tudor façade was added in the 20th century. To the left is Butchery Lane, which was probably a butcher's shambles.

◀ **Cleethorpes**
Beacholme Holiday Camp, The Shop Interior
c1955 C112180
The shop supplies everything a camper could need, from suet for roly-poly pudding to cabbages. Cameras are for hire by the day or week, there are sticks of rock to take home as gifts, and there is a choice of saucy postcards or a local view from the large selection on the rack to the left.

Cleethorpes
The Slipway 1890 26700
The resort flourished in the 1860s when the railway came.
It connected to South Yorkshire for the coal and steel industries,
and it gave the people from the Don Valley towns and Sheffield a
direct rail link. Those who do not want to get their feet wet are
viewing the scene from their carriages.

Cleethorpes, The Beach 1904 51844
A sign at the roadside points to the swimming baths. These began as salt-water baths, and were followed by an open-air bathing pool and later by a modern leisure centre. Beside the slipway, the donkeys are waiting patiently for their small customers. Places to dine and dance dominate the sea front.

Cleethorpes, The Tower 1904 51846
Built in 1902, and known as the Warwick Tower after its creator, it stood about 150 feet high and had a circular lift around a pole in the centre to carry the visitors to the top. The views from the pavilion must have been breathtaking. It was eventually dismantled.

**Cleethorpes
The View from the
Pier 1906** 55732
It is 12 July 1906, and
the thousands of people
on the sea front are
here to celebrate the
opening of the
Kingsway, which was
performed by Lady
Henderson, the wife of
a dignitary of the
railways. The town was
decorated with banners
and bunting for the
occasion. The Kingsway
was to be an esplanade
second to none.

**Cleethorpes
The Pier 1906** 55741
An impressive
pavilion for dancing and
entertainment brought
people flocking to the
1,200ft-long pier,
which was built by
Head Wrightson of
Stockton-on-Tees in
the late 19th century.
The original pavilion
burnt down, and this
one was built about
1904.

◀ **Cleethorpes
The View
from the Big Wheel
c1955** C112135
If the sea wall had not been constructed in 1902, this might have been a very different scene. The huts on the right are selling everything from ice cream to cream and scone teas. There are certainly plenty of customers!

Cleethorpes
The Promenade
and the Beach c1955

C112138

Under the 1902 Cleethorpes Improvement Act, about four acres of land was reclaimed at the foreshore and a sea wall was built. Before this, the sea would splash up to the windows of the houses nearest the shore.

Cleethorpes
Donkey Rides c1960

C112195

A popular entertainment for the children, donkeys arrived on the beaches in the 19th century. As we can see here, they were still popular well into the 20th century. The lady to the left of the view looks as though she is thoroughly enjoying herself.

Spurn Head
The Lighthouse 1899

44753

Situated on a long narrow ridge of sand, the lighthouse has to be monitored for the danger of erosion on its seaward side. Spurn Head lighthouse was built towards the end of the 19th century. Its light was finally extinguished in 1985, with more modern electronic warning devices taking its place.

▼ Easington, High Street c1955 E114511

Some of the groups of cottages here are made with rounded cobbles. Easington Hall, the home of the Overton family, was once situated here, but it fell into ruin many years ago - so did the windmill. There was also a coastguard station here once, but it was closed, and the coastguards moved to Bridlington.

▼ Patrington, Westgate c1955 P184021

Once a minor port on the Humber, the village dates back to 1223. Prosperity declined with the arrival of the railway in 1854. New housing was built in the early 20th century, which brought the village back to life. On the extreme right, the building behind the War Memorial is in use as a garage, advertising petrol.

▲ Withernsea The Donkeys c1955

W177035

Lined up and saddled ready to please the children, donkey rides were a popular form of entertainment on almost every beach. The older girls in the image seem to be dressed in Chinese style, while the little boy to the left favours baggy pants.

◀ **Withernsea**
The Promenade c1955
W177002
Withernsea was labelled in 1890 as 'a dreary watering place'. Its ambitions to become a resort after the arrival of the railway in 1854 were slow to come to fruition. Large houses and a pier were eventually built. The impressive castellated gateway entrance, seen here on the right of the view, is all that now remains of the pier.

Withernsea, Seaside Road c1955 W177009
To the left is Rock Bob the rock shop, and further along are the Carlton Café and Carlton Snack Bar. Above the Kingdom Hall we can see the lighthouse, which was built in 1894. It was erected well back from the coast amongst the houses because of the coastal erosion. Extensions to the sea defence have arrested the erosion for the present.

Withernsea, Queen Street c1955 W177007
This is the main road that leads to a long promenade commanding splendid views out to sea. Note the sign painted on the road for a car park, which was probably used to accommodate the cars of the patrons to the Cosy Cinema - or 'Kinema', as the gilt sign proclaims. The film showing today is 'Destry', starring Audie Murphy.

Churches and Public Houses

The first wooden churches could not withstand the ravages of time, and were replaced by stone buildings that would be altered and added to down the years. Although the wood eventually rotted and disappeared, clues, often in the form of carved stonework, would remain to show to a trained archaeologist's eye that perhaps an earlier house of worship had once stood on the same site. There were vast changes after the Reformation. Churches were often altered dramatically, with walls being knocked down and rebuilt and the interiors undergoing complete facelifts. Some village churches were left to decay because of dwindling attendance and lack of funds, while others have survived by being incorporated into a larger parish and being looked after by a 'mother church'. The Victorians had a passion for churches, and as well as carrying out restorations on existing churches, they also built many new ones.

Carnaby's church of St John the Baptist is a mixture of styles and has an ancient, curiously carved font. All Saint's Church in Hunmanby is believed to have replaced a Saxon church of 1150; the present building has had additions spanning more than six centuries. In the middle of the 19th century, the church was restored and a clock was added, and in 1870 the Admiral's Arch was built in memory of the Lord of Hunmanby Manor. A more recent alteration can be seen at Keyingham Methodist Church. In the 1990s repairs were needed, but funds were short. The cheapest way to solve the problem was to turn the interior of the church around. When marriages take place now, the bride and groom walk up the aisle the other way, and face in the opposite direction when making their vows.

As well as having an ancient church, the village of Skipsea also has a ghost. Legend has it that Drogo, who married King William's niece and built a castle on the land here, fed his wife poison, claiming that it was love

Keyingham, The Methodist Church and Ings Lane c1955 K105014
The village post office often doubled as a general store, as the window-dressing here shows. The church was built in 1846, and is still a well-used and much-loved building. This view has now altered considerably, as the village has expanded over recent years.

potion. He then went to William, asked for a large sum of money, and fled to the continent before his evil deed was discovered. The ghost of his wife is said to haunt Castle Hill to this day.

Whitby Abbey was founded in the 7th century. The ruins that remain, dating from the 11th century, stand high above the harbour as a reminder of the great wealth of the church at that time. Thousands of tourists come to view the ruins and the other historical sites in this beautiful old town.

Many old inns were once coaching inns, used as a stop to change the horses and for the weary travellers to rest and recuperate during the long, uncomfortable coach journeys. Coaching inns were also much used by travelling clergy. Other inns and hotels date from the 19th century, when they were built to accommodate the Victorian tourist. An example is the magnificent Grand Hotel overlooking Scarborough Bay.

By the late 19th and early 20th century, as families and their fortunes died out, some of the large houses that were too expensive to run as private dwellings were sold to be converted into hotels, especially those on the route of the railways. Although much of the railway along the Cleveland Way is now disused, the area is still very popular with cyclists, hikers and people who just want to get close to nature, so many of the country hotels have survived, such as Hayburn Wyke and Cliffemount.

An early beer house would often be just a room in a building or a cottage; it would not have a license to sell spirits, but only beer. The Buck Inn at Hunmanby had a beer house in the middle cottage of a row of three. In the early 20th century the other two cottages were incorporated to make an inn, and in about 1912 a mock-Tudor frontage was added. The Swan Inn stood on the coaching route between Scarborough and Hull, and three times weekly the Wellington and the British Queen coaches would stop and use its facilities. It is believed that the building once stood slightly further back from its present position.

Many of the inns in these images, although modernised internally and standing in altered surroundings, serve their original purpose, which was to beckon and welcome the traveller and to serve them their favourite 'tipple'.

Easington, All Saints' Church and the Tithe Barn c1955 E114513
The village is built up around the church, which had its 800th anniversary in 1990. Many of the villagers celebrated by taking part in a play written by Sheila Yeger, the famous playwright. The tithe barn with its thatched roof dates from the 14th century.

Aldbrough, The George and Dragon c1955 A316012
The name of the village means 'castle' or 'entrenchment'. This quaint public house was probably built on the site of a coaching inn. The present building was constructed in the late 17th century, and it underwent remodelling in the 19th century. It is a focal point of the village.

Hornsea, The Alexandra Hotel c1930 H272082
At the beginning of the 19th century there were only about four hotels in Hornsea, but by the mid 19th century more were built to accommodate the influx of visitors wishing to sea bathe, which was considered to be a cure for minor illnesses and very good for you. This hotel is just beside the North Eastern Railway Station.

▼ **Skipsea, The Village c1955** S399025
We can see All Saints' church to the left in the background of this peaceful scene. King William gave lands here to one of his supporters, Drogo, who built a castle on the land. The ancient earthworks can still be seen.

▼ **Carnaby, The Church c1885** 18015
The church of St John the Baptist is in the village of Carnaby, which is just over two miles from Bridlington and was on the Scarborough and Hull branch of the North Eastern Railway line. The registers date from 1596, and the church has had many alterations over the centuries.

▲ **Hunmanby The Church and the White Swan Hotel c1955** H143010
Many coaching inns were built near to the church because a large proportion of their patrons would have been travelling clergy. Like the White Swan on the left, inns were named so that a sign could be used and recognised by the illiterate. On the right are the tower of All Saint's Church and the Admiral's Arch.

◄ Hunmanby
Bridlington Street c1955

H143005

A chemist and tobacconist stand on the left, while on the right near the parked car is a petrol pump - of course, it would not be allowed so close to buildings now.

The Buck Inn on the corner consists of three cottages joined into one. The name comes from a family called Buck who once lived in the property.

Scarborough South Bay from the Harbour 1897 39459
Overlooking the bay is the magnificent Grand Hotel, built in 1867. There were once cottages on this site, and on 24 May 1849, Anne and Charlotte Bronte arrived to stay in one of the cottages for a holiday. Anne had consumption. She died on 28 May, and is buried at Scarborough.

▼ Cloughton, The Blacksmith's Arms Hotel c1955 C264009

About 200 years old, the hotel stands next to a fully working blacksmith's shop. To the rear of the photograph, we can see the lychgate to St Mary's church. Lychgates were used as a resting place for coffins on entering or leaving the church.

▼ Hayburn Wyke, The Hotel c1960 H517039

Hayburn Wyke is situated about six miles north of Scarborough, and thanks to its tranquil beauty it was popular in the 19th century as a picnic area. Nowadays the area is a lot quieter, and the hotel caters more for walkers hiking across the Cleveland Way.

▲ Whitby East Cliff 1913 66263

Dating back to Roman times, this is the only natural harbour between the Humber and the Tees, and is an important shipping haven. St Mary's church and the ruins of Whitby Abbey stand on the hill overlooking the harbour.

◀ **Lythe**
The Red Lion c1955
L170003
Situated at the top of
Lythe Bank, about four
miles from Whitby, this
charming 17th-century
coaching inn still serves
beer and refreshments to
the public. The picket fence
has gone, and seating
outside is now provided.
The houses to the left are
now painted white.

Ellerby, The Ellerby Hotel c1960 E257061
These buildings date from the 19th century. At that time the group of buildings was a smallholding with a bar. To the far right there was a barn, and the bar was situated to the right of the central farmhouse. Although the interior has now been completely altered, the exterior remains very much as it was in this photo.

Runswick, The Cliffemount Hotel c1960 R71054
Originally built in 1924 as a three-bedroomed house, the building was added to over the following six years to become a hotel. The pavilion to the right is a café that was operated from the garden. The large ball-shaped object to the left is a mine that was eventually removed in 1980.

Staithes
The Cod and Lobster Inn 1927 80216
Ravages of the sea and the storms have been taking their toll over the
centuries. This inn was severely damaged in 1953, and it has been
flooded several times. The sea has destroyed three earlier inns of the
same name, on one occasion during a fierce storm in 1862.

◄ **Aldbrough, The Cliffs and the Beach c1955**

A316006

It is believed that there was once a Saxon settlement nearby that now lies beneath the sea. It was probably destroyed during the 12th or 13th century, when the coastal weather was particularly bad. Here a lady can be seen trying to coax a child down the steps to the beach.

The Villages

Fishing and some agriculture were originally the main livelihoods of the coastal villages. The families worked together. The men went out to sea in their little cobles, and the older boys made lobster pots and mended nets; the women baited the lines, barrelled fish ready for market and collected shellfish, as well as looking after the home and children. Even though the fishing industry has declined and many of the local people now make their living from tourism, the tradition of seamanship lives on. The cobles that were once used to find the best fishing grounds now take visitors on sightseeing trips around the various bays, and the lifeboats are still manned if the need arises.

◄ **Aldbrough, Cross Street c1955** A316010
This street, in one of the largest of the Holderness coastal villages, used to be called Poskett Lane. A mile away there was once a moated castle that had belonged to the landowners, the de Melsa family, which died out in 1377. The village church of St Bartholomew has two tombs and effigies believed to be of the last of the de Melsas.

◄ **Seaton Main Street c1955**
S395009
The houses stand on a hairpin bend of the road that leads to Hornsea. There seem to be more advertisements for cigarettes than anything else here. The white shop front on the left-hand bend is bedecked with them, and the shop on the near right has a sign for Park Drive.

From the middle of the 17th century until 1862, the production of alum gave employment to many. Alum, a chemical used in the tanning industry, was produced from shale in a strange process that involved burning the rock over a long period of time and then pouring human urine over the rocks. The urine was brought in by boat from all over England. Throughout the 19th century, jet was another commodity that the landscape provided. The semi-precious stone was mined from the cliffs, and craftsmen in Whitby would fashion it into jewellery and ornaments. The industry declined in the 1920s, owing to cheaper imports being brought in. The ancient craft is kept alive, although on a much smaller scale: jet is still carved and sold in Whitby. The area around the cliff villages still shows the remains of the workings of the alum and jet industry.

Until the early years of the 19th century, the Yorkshire coast was rife with smuggling. It began in the 14th century, when the export of wool was banned; as the years went on, high taxes were imposed on incoming goods, such as tea, coffee, gin, silk and many other items. The rugged coastline, criss-crossed with gullies and valleys between high cliffs, and bays with smooth beaches where a small boat could be easily landed away from prying eyes, made it ideal for the illicit trade. The smugglers made huge profits on their cargo, so they could afford to pay the skippers of large sailing vessels well, and also the seaman and labourers. Every class of people bought the goods, from the poorer working classes to the rich landowners and the gentry. Even the clergy were sometimes involved. Because so many people benefited from the trade, it was rare that information on the smugglers would be given to the preventive men, even if a reward were offered. Many smugglers were never caught, but the ones that were might pay dearly. Sometimes they faced transportation, were imprisoned, sent for a term in one of the forces or even condemned to death, usually by hanging. It was not until the 1820s, when the coastguards became more efficient and duty on goods was lowered, that smuggling declined.

There are many stories and legends of smugglers using

Atwick, Cliff Lane c1960 A172010
The small village is built around the village green. There is an inn, some shops and the remains of the old market cross. Over the centuries, the sea has crept steadily closer to the village and is now only a few hundred yards away.

caves, hidden cupboards and secret tunnels, which sometimes covered a long distance, to transport and hide the contraband. These are certainly not all tall tales. Many of the villages have been built in a higgledy-piggledy fashion clinging to the side of cliffs. Houses were built close together, and were often intertwined with connecting cellars; in fact in Robin Hoods Bay, or Baytown as it was known, it was said that 'a bale of silk could pass from the bottom of the village to the top without seeing daylight'. Sad to say, owing to erosion hundreds of houses have been lost in Robin Hood's Bay and the other coastal villages that were built near the shoreline or on the sides of the cliffs over the centuries. Ravenscar was reputed to be where King George III was treated for his bouts of insanity. Peak House, as it was then known, was the home of the Reverend Doctor Frank Willis, who owned an asylum in Lincolnshire that King George attended. The treatments consisted of bleeding with leeches and immersing in cold water amongst other rather barbaric medical practices. Not much in the way of a cure by modern standards! Doctor Willis was said to have later lost his house in a gamble over a race between two woodlice running over a saucer. Ancient churches, old inns, historic houses (many now in use as hotels) and the different architectural styles that have developed

Atwick
The Cliffs c1960 A172005
Erosion is a real problem here, and it can be quite difficult to get down to the beach. However, judging by the parked cars and caravans, the visitors are quite happy just to look at the magnificent view over the cliff top.

Skipsea
The Green c1960 S399020
As a lady opens her gate to enter the grounds of the attractive house, she turns to watch the little tot on his tricycle about to ride over the green, perhaps to make sure he is being supervised.

▼ **Beeford, Main Street c1955** B664017

This is a peaceful village scene, with an inn on the far right of the wide road. Visitors come here to see the lovely 15th-century church of St Leonard. On the chancel floor is a brass portrait of a rector of the 15th century, Thomas Tonge.

▼ **Ulrome, Top View Stores c1955** U34059

A large platform with huge oak supporting piles was discovered here in 1880. It is believed to have been a dwelling that once stood upon a lake, perhaps in the Bronze Age. The end house is in use as a shop, which would have served the caravan park on the land next to it.

▲ **Barmston South Cliff Bungalows c1955** B850037

On a fine summer's day, these bungalows must have looked ideal to the prospective buyer with clean sea air and a beautiful view. Sad to say, Neptune claimed them one by one in the 1970s.

◄ **Barmston**
The Village c1955 B850058
This, the main part of the
village, is built far enough
inland to be safe from
the ravages of the sea. The
Boynton family had a large
influence here; they built a
fine hall with a moated
enclosure, of which some
parts still remain.

▼ **Burton Agnes, The Hall 1908** 59908
This late Elizabethan house is filled with treasures, including fine works of art. The descendants of the original family still occupy the building. The large statue in the centre of the view is a gladiator wielding his sword.

▼ **Sewerby, Cliff Walk c1955** S396004
In 1779, the peace of this tiny village was shattered by the noise of gunfire when the ships of the Royal Navy and the ships of the United States came together in the Battle of Flamborough Head. Nowadays, the loudest noise is the sound of the waves crashing against the cliffs in severe weather.

▲ **Sewerby
The Park Gateway
c1955** S396005
The gate leads to 50 acres of parkland surrounding Sewerby Hall, which was built between 1714 and 1720. The estate was bought by Bridlington Corporation and opened to the public in 1936. The house contains beautiful period rooms and the Museum of East Yorkshire.

◀ **Sewerby**
The View towards
Bridlington c1955 S396002
Named by the Danes,
Sewerby has had different
spellings, including Sewarby
and Suerby. Many Roman
artifacts have been found in
the area. Even before the
Danes, Iron Age man built a
huge earthwork known as
Danes Dyke.

▼ **Flamborough, Flamborough Head 1888** 21408

Many a vessel has come to grief while trying to round the head to the safe harbour of Bridlington. The crews of the lifeboats here have their work cut out in bad weather when ships have got into difficulties. The name Flamborough is Norse, and means 'settlement on a headland'.

▼ **Flamborough, North Landing 1908** 59912

Villagers wait for the herring boats to come in with their catches. There were 30 fishing boats here in the middle of the 19th century, but by the end of the First World War they were nearly all gone. Treacherous seas have claimed many lives here, and the graveyards are full of drowned seafarers.

▲ **Flamborough The Boating Station c1930** F30007

Here we have another view of North Landing, showing the brick-built lifeboat house. The crew will have returned to this bay cold, wet and tired, sometimes full of satisfaction because lives will have been saved, but other times they will have returned with bodies.

◀ **Flamborough
The King and Queen
Rocks 1927** 80145
As with many natural rock
formations along the coast,
the wind and sea sometimes
takes its toll - the King Rock
has now collapsed. About a
mile away, another pair of
twin stacks, named Adam
and Eve, stood at Selwick
Bay: Eve suffered the same
fate as the King and
collapsed.

Flamborough
South Landing c1930 F30051
A lifeboat station was established here in 1871 as well as the one
at North Landing, because the curve of the cliff gave shelter and made it easier
to launch a boat from here. The station closed in 1938.

Flamborough
The Lighthouse c1940 F30063
The lighthouse was designed by Samuel Watts and built by John Matson at a cost of £8000.
It was first lit on 1 December 1806. Originally oil burning, it was modified to electricity in 1940,
about the time that this photo was taken. It was modified further in 1974.

▼ **Flamborough, The Village c1950** F30107

The village had a very tight-knit, private community. Sword dances, Morris dances and superstition were a village way of life until the end of the 19th century. If a fisherman was baiting his line, he would think it unlucky if a fox, hare, rabbit or pig were mentioned, and he would abandon his fishing for that day.

◄ **Bempton
The Cliffs 1908** 59910

Because these forbidding, almost vertical cliffs are chalk, erosion through time from the sea and wind has left little 'pockets' in the cliff face, which make it an ideal situation for birds: indeed, it is the largest bird breeding ground in Britain. An estimated 200,000 birds of many different species nest here.

▲ **Reighton
The Gap, Speeton
Cliffs c1955** R239016

The sea looks calm and peaceful in this photograph. But in 1935, a vessel (the 'Skegness') got into difficulties and ran onto the cliffs. The weather conditions were so bad that the would-be rescuers had to stand by helplessly and watch the entire crew die.

◄ **Reighton**
The Gap c1955 R239018
Caravans stretch for as far as the eye can see. Now, holiday parks with modern amenities take up this land. Nearby stands Reighton Hall, which was built in 1735. The Hall has had many uses, including being a boys' school and a home for evacuees during the war. It is now a hotel.

◀ **Hunmanby**
The Cross c1955   H143007
The name of the village
comes from 'Hudemanebi',
a Scandinavian word
meaning 'the farm of dog
keepers'. A weekly market
was held here until the 18th
century, and this medieval
market cross stands on
Cross Hill.

◄ Reighton
The Gap c1965 R239051
Situated at the southern end of Filey's long beach, the outcrop of Flamborough Head can be seen in the distance. Judging by the way the sand is churned up, the little horse has had a few gallops up and down. The boy with his hands in his pockets seems fascinated by the animal.

◄ Cayton Bay
The Holiday Camp c1960
C260006
Situated between Filey and Scarborough, this is an ideal place for a holiday. Now there are modern holiday camps here, including Cayton Bay and Killerby Old Hall estate, which has a wildlife lake. Rumour has it that there was once a smuggler's tunnel leading inland from Killerby Hall.

Cayton Bay ▶
The Cliffs and the Beach
c1960 C260005
The wide, low-lying, sandy beach here was formed by structural faults. The five-mile cliff-top walk between here and Filey is a geologist's dream: it is made up from many rock types formed in the Jurassic period.

▼ **Cayton Bay, The Beach c1960**
C260002
Even the dog looks as though it is enjoying itself, and the donkeys are certainly keeping busy on this beautiful beach. The village is small; it has a 12th-century church dedicated to John the Baptist.

▲ **Cloughton, Wyke c1955**
C264037
This rocky inlet is reputed to have been used by smugglers. It was said that there was a secret tunnel from here leading to the manor house. The area was once known as Clotune, and was in the manor of Walsgrave. A sandstone quarry above the village is the source of the stone for Scarborough Castle.

◄ **Hayburn Wyke
The Waterfall c1960**
H517035
A small wooden bridge
across Hayburn Beck
leads to the rocky
beach, where the stream
cascades over large
gritstone boulders into a
pool on the beach
below. We may be
thankful that this is now
a protected nature
reserve.

◀ **Hayburn Wyke
The View Looking
North c1960** H517004
A wide variety of wildlife
and plants are to be
found around the
undercliff. This family
has the beach all to
themselves; what are
they searching for?
Perhaps crabs or small
fish left by the tide.

▼ **Staintondale
The Camping Coaches c1960**
S333008
The end of an era for the
railway: the coaches on the
disused line would have made
very large and comfortable
holiday homes. Nowadays there
are modern holiday villages
here with streamlined caravans,
cottages and chalets all around
this lovely area. Nearby there is
now a large shire horse farm.

◀ **Staintondale
The Village c1960**
S333013
During the reign of
King Stephen in the
12th century, the
original owners of Bell
Hill Farm, Staintondale,
rang a bell or blew a
horn every evening to
act as a guide to
travellers. As payment,
the villagers were
exempt from market and
road tolls.

▼ **Ravenscar, Station Square 1901** 46802

The estate here was sold to a development company in 1895, and the intention was to build a large resort. The company was assailed by financial difficulties in 1913, and very few houses were ever completed. Billboards on the side of the Station Square shop advertise land for sale, and the board on the fence advertises the same for Robin Hoods Bay.

▼ **Ravenscar, Station Square c1960** R11007

Mention of a Roman signal station in the Domesday Book in 1086 dates the history of this area back as far as the fourth century. This view shows that the houses are still few and far between, and the village, known as 'the town that never was', remains much the same now.

▲ **Ravenscar Ravenhall Road c1960**

R11015

A gentleman stands at the door of Crag Hill House, perhaps calling over to the man walking his dog. Two children sit by the roadside playing near the sign for a café. It seems hard to believe that this was once an industrial landscape - alum used to be mined here.

◀ **Ravenscar**
The Cliffs 1901 46801
The undercliff, in medieval times, was named Darn Cliff, meaning 'hidden cliff'. With views like this, no wonder there was a dream of a resort being built. One house that did reach completion and has splendid views was Cliff House.

▼ **Ravenscar, The Railway c1960** R11004

The railway arrived here in 1884. So that W H Hammond, who bought Raven Hall and became a local benefactor, did not have to look at an ugly railway line, a tunnel was constructed. Because the tunnel was often wet and on a steep gradient, it sometimes took several efforts for the trains to continue on their journey.

▼ **Robin Hoods Bay, The Town 1901** 46794

Situated on precarious cliffs, the town has suffered greatly from erosion over the years. The narrow, twisting streets and quaint buildings attract artists and photographers from all over the world to come and immortalise its beauty.

▲ **Robin Hoods Bay New Road c1955** R41054

At the bottom of Chapel Street, visitors ready for a stay in the nearby hotel unload their suitcases from a cart. We can see the steepness of the streets by comparing the level of the Laurel Inn with the houses rising up behind.

◀ **Saltwick Bay**
Black Nab 1913 66297
This is one of the dark, forbidding formations of rock that are to be seen along this coast. One has to be careful while walking along the cliff top because of the severe erosion that is taking place. In fact, in some places the path has been moved back from the edge.

▼ **Saltwick Bay, The Holiday Camp, North Field c1960** S810165
This site looks almost deserted, except for a Volkswagen parked by
one of the caravans and a few cows grazing in the field behind. The
town of Whitby can be seen in the distance, with the ruins of Whitby
Abbey dominating the skyline.

▼ **Sandsend, East Row 1901** 46810
A horse and cart trundles along the road spanning East Beck, one of
two streams that meander through the village - the other is Sandsend
Beck. Much of the village still retains much of its original charm.

▲ **Sandsend
East Row 1925** 78989
In the 12th century,
Sandsend was recorded
as having 53 tenants'
cottages belonging to the
lord of the manor. The
area is known as Dunsley
Bay, and Sandsend is
really two villages. These
old red-roofed houses on
East Row are the first we
reach if we are coming
from Whitby.

◀ **Sandsend
The Village 1925** 77728
The village reached
prosperity in the 17th
century with the discovery
of alum, which was used in
the dying and tanning
industry. The alum mines
gave employment until
1867, a span of more than
250 years. There are still
many traces of the workings
of the alum mines nearby.

◄ **Sandsend
Kettleness Point 1925**
78987
The village of Kettleness
succumbed to disaster
on 17 December 1829
when the cliff broke
away and the houses
and alum works fell into
the sea. Fortunately, the
alum ship 'Little Henry'
managed to take the
villagers to safety and no
lives were lost.

Sandsend
Meadow Fields and Kettleness
Nab 1925 77726
Sandsend is about three miles from Whitby, situated at the mouth of Sandsend Wyke; the village is almost hidden from view because of the mighty cliffs and Mulgrave Wood nearby. In the woods are ancient earthworks, the remains of Mulgrave Castle, which dates from the 13th century.

Sandsend
The Beach 1925 78992
The beach huts show that this was and still is a popular beach. Most of the larger houses have been converted to hotels to cater for the hundreds of tourists that arrive every summer. I wonder how the two children are to get their little boat back without wading into the water!

Lythe
The Village c1965
L170009
Situated on a steep hill on a road that comes from Sandsend, the village has a Saxon church; here are buried the bodies of seven unidentified sailors that were washed up on the tides.

Runswick
From the Beach c1885 18200
The older houses of this charming little village, like many others on this coast, are built hanging precariously onto a cliff. The villagers once relied almost solely on fishing. There would have to be a high tide before these little cobles could be launched.

Runswick
The Bay 1927 80197
The steep, winding stairs and the difference in levels of the houses show how the buildings cling to the steep cliff, the summit of which rises high above. To the right of the cottage are crates with small holes in them; perhaps this was the home of a pigeon fancier!

Runswick
The Beach 1929 82490
Jet mining was a large industry here, and involved cutting into the
cliff. Craftsmen who manufactured it into beautiful ornaments and
jewellery bought the jet. In the cliff that was used for the mine
there was a cave, Hob Holes: legend had it that a hob man, or
goblin, lived there who could cure whooping cough.

Runswick, The Bay 1936 87341
Whalers, fishermen and smugglers were once regular visitors to the bay. Erosion has always been a problem here.
In 1682, a landslide destroyed every dwelling except one. No lives were lost, as the village was evacuated in time.
Another landslide in 1858 demolished an iron smelting works.

Runswick, The Village 1927 80204
This picturesque view shows how far out the tide would recede. The road leading up the cliff from the village looks a steep, arduous walk. To the far left of the road, a lone camper has pitched a tent on a piece of grassy land.

Runswick, The Beach c1965 R71077
To the front of the view is the lifeboat house and boat park. The lifeboat was once crewed by women when the men of the crew were caught in a squall. Severe weather conditions were still causing problems here at this time, but in 1970 a sea wall was built that will protect the village in the future.

▼ **Staithes, Penny Nab c1885** 18213
This view and view No 79002 show how Staithes nestles in the shadow of the two mighty cliffs. The stream flows through the village, and is crossed by a sturdy replacement to what was once a wooden bridge.

▼ **Staithes, Cowbar Nab 1925** 79002
The village takes its name from the staith that has been repaired and reinforced to remain its main defence against the unpredictable North Sea for centuries. This view shows how close the buildings are to disaster when a severe storm strikes.

▲ **Staithes
Seaton Garth 1927**
80215
This is probably the oldest part of the present village. The houses were built on a fair sized, flat piece of land sheltered by Penny Nab. There was easy access to and from the sea for the cobles. To the centre of the image, a cat scrounges, perhaps for left-over fish.

◀ **Staithes**
The Beach c1955 S176032
A sign on one of the boats advertises sea trips, and the 'Frank and Elizabeth, the 'Sunbeam' and another craft seem to be quite busy. A couple, the lady wearing a bathing cap, are making the most of the weather by having a dip in the ocean.

▼ Staithes, The Village 1932 85269
This narrow, winding street leads to the Cod and Lobster Inn and the sea. Yards or passages lead to many of the houses; they seem to have been put wherever they would fit, a little like a wrongly-completed jigsaw. This gives the village a unique charm.

▼ Staithes, High Street c1955 S176026
In the summer months, this street is congested with cars. Much of the villagers' living comes from the tourist trade, a far cry from the century before, when the men risked their lives going out to sea in their small boats and women spent their time looking after the home and family, as well as helping their menfolk with the nets and lines.

▲ Staithes Fishwives c1960
S176105
When the village relied almost entirely on fishing for a living, it would be the women who baited the lines, usually with mussels, or sometimes limpets. Here, with the bridge that links the two sides of the village in the background, are four women showing off their selection of crabs.

◄ **Staithes**
Captain Cook's Cottage c1955
S176036
The young James Cook was sent by his father to Staithes from Great Ayton to serve an apprenticeship to a grocer and haberdasher, Mr Sanderson. The call of the sea must have been too much for him, for within a year he had left to go to Whitby and embark on what became a famous career.

▲ **Hornsea**
Seaton Road c1950
H272078
Many of the houses in
this area, some around
300 years old, were built
of stones and pebbles.
The town hosts a
museum in what was
once a farmhouse, and
the Victorian era returns
with local people
demonstrating bygone
crafts.

The Towns

From the Humber Estuary to Bridlington the coast is quite flat, with unbroken, sandy beaches. The chalk cliff of Flamborough Head juts out over Bridlington Bay, giving it some protection from the fierce northerly winds. Hornsea is situated midway between Flamborough Head and Spurn Point. The name means 'the horn shaped lake'; this refers to the large freshwater lake known as the Mere, which brings thousands of tourists each year to enjoy the birds that frequent it. Boating and fishing can be enjoyed at the Mere as well. In the reign of Henry III, a dispute took place between the monastery of Meaux in France and the Abbey of St Mary at York over the fishing rights of the Mere: a trial by battle followed, and St Mary's won.

Hornsea is also the home of the famous Hornsea Pottery. The church of St Nicholas was built of cobblestones in the 14th century. Under the chancel lies a vaulted crypt that was reputed to have been used for stashing contraband brought in by smugglers. A pirate who had murdered his captain on a ship off the Hornsea coast was caught and executed in London. His body was brought to Hornsea and hung on the gallows as a warning to other pirates.

◀ **Hornsea**
The Mere c1950
H272127
Joseph Wade, a Hull timber merchant, had a strong influence on the development of a resort here following the arrival of the railway in 1864. Before this, a hotel and some large lodging houses were already catering for people visiting the attractive inland mere to take advantage of the boating and fishing.

Bridlington was originally divided into two parts: the quay, where the fishermen lived in their cottages, and the area that centered round a monastery. The arrival of the railway, and with it the Victorian tourist, saw buildings spring up in between the two. The present 'Brid', as it is fondly known, has two piers, both built in the 19th century, which the fishermen still work from; a very pleasant promenade; and all the traditional seaside attractions.

Filey once had a Roman signal station, one of a line of sites that included Flamborough, Ravenscar and Scarborough. The bay here forms a natural harbour, and Filey was a farming and fishing community. Records show that a market started up here in 1221. A spa was discovered in about 1670, and this and the attractions of the seaside brought visitors. In the 1840s, John Wilkes Unett purchased land on the cliff top and began building the Crescent. By the 1860s, Filey was considered very fashionable as a resort. Today, although it is perhaps not as busy as some resorts, Filey remains a very pleasant seaside town.

This coast, especially from where the cliffs begin, was a rugged protection against invasion. Fortresses and castles could be built at strategic points on the high ground, giving a view many miles out to sea and inland. The ruins of Scarborough Castle still stand to remind us of these great feats of fortified building. Standing some 300 feet above the harbour below, for five centuries the castle was an important base for royalty. Over these centuries it was added to and improved. The castle has withstood many a siege throughout the ages, but has only been severely damaged twice: once during the Civil War, and then in 1914 when it was attacked by German battle cruisers. The Victorians brought continued prosperity to Scarborough, and it became known as 'the queen of watering places'. Many of the large 19th-century buildings survive, giving the town an air of grandeur; but the sea front is now packed with amusement arcades, bingo halls and cafes, rather than the genteel entertainments that the Victorians enjoyed.

Hornsea, The Floral Hall c1950 H272108
In the early 18th century, visitors were attracted here because of the three springs in the area, one very near this hall. Spa water was considered very therapeutic. The hall is still used as a venue for entertainments. The billboards here advertise 'Show Time' and a photographic competition.

Religious orders also used the Yorkshire coast to build their abbeys and churches. Whitby Abbey is a prime example. Built originally in the 7th century, it was almost entirely rebuilt in the 13th and 14th centuries, and it is the ruins of this later structure that can be seen today. Even though there is little left now, the remains are an awe-inspiring, haunting reminder of the magnificent grandeur of this once proud building.

Saltburn-by-the-Sea was created because of one man's dream. In 1861 Henry Pease, a Quaker, who was a director of the Stockton and Darlington Railway, seeing the cliff above the tiny fishing hamlet, persuaded his family that this would make an ideal resort, and so the railway was extended to Saltburn. He built a grand hotel to cater for the wealthy, and thus 'New' Saltburn was born. The town still has a hint of exclusiveness. Its water-balance cliff-top lift and the newly-renovated pier help the town to hold on to its 19th-century roots. A Victorian festival is held every year: the locals dress in period costume, and there are entertainments and events to enjoy.

Hornsea
Cliff Road c1950 H272096
Winifred Holtby lived in this road while she was writing her novel 'South Riding'. Another famous visitor to the town was Lawrence of Arabia, who frequently visited the White Cottage in the Eastgate area. A signpost on the corner of the wide road points to the sea, and the Clifton Guest House stands opposite.

Hornsea
The Beach c1950 H272072
Hornsea Pottery is famous worldwide, and collectors pay a considerable amount for some of the older pieces. In this view, holidaymakers are enjoying cheaper pleasures. The dressing tents are set up, the deckchairs are hired and the picnic baskets are opened for an enjoyable day on the beach.

**Bridlington
The New Spa and the
Bandstand 1897**
39369
Built in 1896, this was
a popular entertainment
and meeting place. A
military band plays in
the bandstand. The
fashionable ladies sitting
on a bench listening
have their hats tied on
with veils, perhaps to
stop the sea breeze
carrying them off.

Bridlington
The New Spa 1903 50015
The marketplace here was probably laid out in the 13th century,
and some of the buildings in the Old Town are 17th-century.
This promenade was laid out to attract the Victorian visitor, and the
town was noted for its beautiful flowerbeds. On the left we can just
see a small part of a rockery.

Bridlington
The Sands 1926 79015
Ice cream and tea are for sale further along the beach. The stall in
the centre seems to be selling bottled drinks and perhaps biscuits.
The tent to the front of the view advertises moderate fees to
consult a palmist and clairvoyant.

◄ **Bridlington
The Harbour 1913** 66244
The Quay and the harbour
were once separate from
the rest of the town. The
present harbour walls date
from the middle of the
19th century; they are
built on the site of previous
medieval walls. To the left,
on the pier, there is a large
telescope with which the
flurry of little boats could be
viewed.

◀ Bridlington
The Harbour 1903
50022

Trawlers still go deep-sea fishing and keelboats pot fishing from here as they have done for longer than anyone can remember. As well as fishing boats, there are many little boats and yachts available to take visitors for a cruise round the bay.

Bridlington ▶
Rough Sea
South Side 1906
55764a

The south pier was completed in 1848. During the winter months these rough seas are common on this coast. A terrible storm in 1871 claimed the lives of six local lifeboat men. In the summer months the pier would attract hundreds of people.

◀ Bridlington
SS 'Yorkshireman' c1940
B206179

In May 1928, this vessel started service in Bridlington, and except for the war years she spent every summer at the town. She could carry up to 400 passengers on her sea excursions. During the winter she did towing work on the Humber. She was finally towed to Belgium in 1954 and was broken up in 1965.

**Bridlington
The Royal Hall
Interior 1927** 80136
This beautiful hall was
destroyed by fire in
1932, but within only
five months a
replacement had been
built. The railway arrived
here from Hull in 1846,
and brought with it
many visitors from all
over Yorkshire, so
entertainment venues
were important.

Filey, Primrose Valley c1935 F23099
Don't the girls look just the thing with their skirts spread out around them on the grass! Billy Butlin bought the land here and opened one of his holiday camps in 1945. In 1995, just beside the old Butlin camp, the modern chalets of Primrose Valley Holiday Camp were built.

Filey, The Sands 1927 80157
Children fish for small marine life in the pools the tide has left behind. The large, gracious, Victorian terraces serving as guesthouses and hotels dominate the skyline along the sea front. The building of the new town began in 1840, and by 1867 it was a bustling resort.

Filey
The Sands 1932 85311
Andie Craine and his Pierrots are doing their show on the beach.
Their performances began in 1846 and continued for 46 years.
In 1910 they opened the Alfresco Pavilion, and eventually they
became known as the Royal Filey Pierrots. Andie died in 1944
and is buried at Filey.

Filey
The Beach c1935
F23088
Andie and his Pierrots
are performing again.
Their poster proclaims
'on with the show', and
they have attracted a
large crowd, some
watching from the ledge
in front of the band-
stand. A bit of decorum
is being practised,
judging by the amount
of bathing or 'dressing'
tents that are set up.

◀ **Filey**
The Promenade c1960
F23178
No road signs or parking restrictions here. The tea stall and the small Walls ice cream stall are doing a roaring trade. There are swing boats and roundabouts for the little ones. Some of the visitors are taking a boat trip out on the bay, while others are enjoying a paddle in the calm sea.

◀ **Filey**
The Parade 1932 85308
Walking along with their
sun-bonneted charges,
these three ladies have a
wonderful view of the bay.
The long promontory of
Filey Brigg, part of a huge
curve of cliffs, shelters this
long stretch of firm beach
from the worst of the north-
east gales. A new parade
was constructed in 1955.

▼ **Filey**
Fishing c1945 F23103
What an ideal way to
spend a relaxing
afternoon. A gentleman
with a fishing line tries his
luck in the ocean, while
the children search the
seaweed-covered rocks
for anything they can find.
The cliffs and rocks on
either side of Filey form a
sheltered bay.

◀ **Filey**
The Ravine c1935
F23086
Until the 19th century
this was a boundary
between the north and
east ridings. There were
also a stream and small
pools here, which were
eventually covered in to
form part of the sewer.
Before the onslaught of
the motorcar, a carriage
road was laid and
flowers and trees were
planted, making it a
beauty spot.

**Scarborough
The Bay 1886** 18240
The Victorians loved all
sorts of entertainment,
especially music.
Travelling showmen
were a common sight.
Here the 'nigger
minstrels' seem to
be collecting money
from the crowd
standing on the beach
waiting for the show to
begin.

Scarborough, The Beach c1955 S71148
In the shadow of the Lord Nelson Hotel and the lifeboat house, a century on from the first day-trippers, some of the surroundings have altered, fashions have changed and deckchairs are in abundance, but the beach still attracts huge crowds every season.

Scarborough, From the Fish Pier 1890 23465
One of the boats on the right has the mark PZ, so she may have come from Penzance, a very long journey! Fishing, once the livelihood of many, had declined by the early 20th century, so small boats are now mainly used to take visitors trips around the bay.

Scarborough
The Bay c1885 18233
The large spa building in the centre of the view was rebuilt in 1877
after a catalogue of disasters. It was damaged by storms in 1808,
1825 and 1836. After repair in 1856, it was gutted by fire in 1876.
The hall is now used as a venue for different entertainments.

Scarborough
The Spa Promenade
1890 23452
In 1620, Elizabeth
Farrow claimed that the
spa water here was
beneficial to health. This
attracted the wealthy,
and so began the
town's development.
This was probably the
earliest seaside resort
in the country. When
the first train arrived
here in July 1845, it
brought with it the
day-trippers.

Scarborough, The Lighthouse 1890 23470
This lighthouse was built on St Vincent's Pier in 1810, but it was destroyed during a German raid on 17 December 1914. A replacement was erected in 1931. The vessel moored at the pier displays the complex rigging for the sails of the old sailing ships.

Scarborough, The View from North Cliff c1955 S71091
The tram lift saves a long, tiring climb to the top of the hill. An early form of people carrier, a charabanc, is parked towards the sea wall, while a double-decker bus has stopped to let the day-trippers alight. At the moment the tide is in, but later on the beach will be thronged with people.

Scarborough, Saint Nicholas Cliff 1890 23476A
This party of visitors have a wonderful view from a lookout over the bay, even though there is a mist. Large Victorian residences can be seen on the clifftop. The people seem to be dressed in their Sunday best, with the men sporting top hats and the ladies fashionable bonnets. Note the large wheels on the perambulator.

Scarborough, The Castle c1955 S71107
Even though only the ruins of the keep and the barbican remain, it is obvious how strong this fortress once was. One can conjure up visions of the Romans, Vikings, kings and queens that have occupied the castle throughout the centuries.

Whitby, 'Gemini' 1891 28862
The only thing twin-like about these little girls is the very bad-tempered scowl on their faces. They certainly are not saying 'cheese'. Perhaps they didn't like the photographer - or it might be the fact that they are sitting on a rock covered in wet seaweed.

Whitby, Church Steps 1913 66284
Known locally as Jacob's Ladder, the original steps dated back six hundred years. Coffins would have been carried from the town below up to the church. The young lady on the right looking rather pensive is perhaps wondering whether she should continue climbing the 199 steps or return to the bottom.

Whitby
The Bridge 1923 74316
Linking the east and west sides of the town over the River Esk,
the bridge is now crammed with tourists in the summer months.
Captain Cook was apprenticed here at the age of seventeen; there
are many monuments to him here, including a statue and the
Captain Cook Museum.

Whitby, Watching the Fishing Fleet c1955 W81148
Whaling ships once departed from here to sail to the Arctic in search of a catch. When whaling declined, herring became important to the town's prosperity; but the herring fishery is now all but gone, and the town relies mainly on tourism.

Whitby, Larpool Viaduct 1884 18170
The viaduct was originally erected for the Scarborough and Whitby Railway. The first brick was laid in 1882 and the first locomotive crossed the thirteen-arched viaduct in 1884. Trains from Scarborough crossed the viaduct, stopped at West Cliff and then reversed steeply down beneath the viaduct into Whitby.

◀ **Saltburn-by-the-Sea
Old Saltburn 1923**

74274

This, the original hamlet on the shore, consisted of fishermen's cottages and the Ship and Nimrod Inns. Henry Pease was said to have had a vision of 'a town arisen on the edge of a cliff'. He was then instrumental in founding 'New' Saltburn on the top of the cliff in 1861.

▼ **Saltburn-by-the-Sea, The Italian Gardens 1923** 74275

Gardens such as this were once a common feature. This beautiful display has survived, but vandalism and lack of funds has meant that many have disappeared. To the back of the image is the Halfpenny Bridge, so named because of the toll charged to cross. Built in 1869, it was demolished in 1974 against locals' and conservationists' wishes.

▲ **Saltburn-by-the-Sea
The Pier Entrance
1913** 66354

Built in 1884, this water-balance cliff lift is the oldest in Britain that is still in use. The pier, which is the only one of six along the Yorkshire coast to have survived, has just undergone a massive renovation in the hope that it will now survive at least another 100 years.

◄ **Saltburn-by-the-Sea
Windy Cliff Sands 1932**
85287
The little beach huts and
tearooms look cosy enough
sheltering under the cliff,
but as the name implies it
would be a different
matter on the cliff top.
There is a breathtaking walk
of fifty miles along these
cliffs from Saltburn to Filey.
Recommended only in
clement weather!

Saltburn-by-the-Sea, From the East 1932 85277
One can imagine the smugglers being able to transport their contraband from the shore, up the rugged terrain and inland without being detected, before these roads were built. The landlord of the Ship Inn situated in the old hamlet was John Andrews, who was notorious for his smuggling.

Saltburn-by-the-Sea, The Grotto 1932 85290
This little folly was built as a shelter where one could rest and look out onto the well-laid-out flowerbeds. It was erected in the early 1930s in concrete with limestone facing. Sad to say, it is in a state of disrepair owing to vandalism and neglect; the local history society are trying to have improvements made to the whole area.

Index

Frith Book Co Titles

www.francisfrith.co.uk

The Frith Book Company publishes over 100 new titles each year. A selection of those currently available are listed below. For latest catalogue please contact Frith Book Co.

Town Books 96 pages, approx 100 photos. County and Themed Books 128 pages, approx 150 photos (unless specified). All titles hardback laminated case and jacket except those indicated pb (paperback)

Title	ISBN	Price
Amersham, Chesham & Rickmansworth (pb)	1-85937-340-2	£9.99
Ancient Monuments & Stone Circles	1-85937-143-4	£17.99
Aylesbury (pb)	1-85937-227-9	£9.99
Bakewell	1-85937-113-2	£12.99
Barnstaple (pb)	1-85937-300-3	£9.99
Bath (pb)	1-85937419-0	£9.99
Bedford (pb)	1-85937-205-8	£9.99
Berkshire (pb)	1-85937-191-4	£9.99
Berkshire Churches	1-85937-170-1	£17.99
Blackpool (pb)	1-85937-382-8	£9.99
Bognor Regis (pb)	1-85937-431-x	£9.99
Bournemouth	1-85937-067-5	£12.99
Bradford (pb)	1-85937-204-x	£9.99
Brighton & Hove(pb)	1-85937-192-2	£8.99
Bristol (pb)	1-85937-264-3	£9.99
British Life A Century Ago (pb)	1-85937-213-9	£9.99
Buckinghamshire (pb)	1-85937-200-7	£9.99
Camberley (pb)	1-85937-222-8	£9.99
Cambridge (pb)	1-85937-422-0	£9.99
Cambridgeshire (pb)	1-85937-420-4	£9.99
Canals & Waterways (pb)	1-85937-291-0	£9.99
Canterbury Cathedral (pb)	1-85937-179-5	£9.99
Cardiff (pb)	1-85937-093-4	£9.99
Carmarthenshire	1-85937-216-3	£14.99
Chelmsford (pb)	1-85937-310-0	£9.99
Cheltenham (pb)	1-85937-095-0	£9.99
Cheshire (pb)	1-85937-271-6	£9.99
Chester	1-85937-090-x	£12.99
Chesterfield	1-85937-378-x	£9.99
Chichester (pb)	1-85937-228-7	£9.99
Colchester (pb)	1-85937-188-4	£8.99
Cornish Coast	1-85937-163-9	£14.99
Cornwall (pb)	1-85937-229-5	£9.99
Cornwall Living Memories	1-85937-248-1	£14.99
Cotswolds (pb)	1-85937-230-9	£9.99
Cotswolds Living Memories	1-85937-255-4	£14.99
County Durham	1-85937-123-x	£14.99
Croydon Living Memories	1-85937-162-0	£9.99
Cumbria	1-85937-101-9	£14.99
Dartmoor	1-85937-145-0	£14.99
Derby (pb)	1-85937-367-4	£9.99
Derbyshire (pb)	1-85937-196-5	£9.99
Devon (pb)	1-85937-297-x	£9.99
Dorset (pb)	1-85937-269-4	£9.99
Dorset Churches	1-85937-172-8	£17.99
Dorset Coast (pb)	1-85937-299-6	£9.99
Dorset Living Memories	1-85937-210-4	£14.99
Down the Severn	1-85937-118-3	£14.99
Down the Thames (pb)	1-85937-278-3	£9.99
Down the Trent	1-85937-311-9	£14.99
Dublin (pb)	1-85937-231-7	£9.99
East Anglia (pb)	1-85937-265-1	£9.99
East London	1-85937-080-2	£14.99
East Sussex	1-85937-130-2	£14.99
Eastbourne	1-85937-061-6	£12.99
Edinburgh (pb)	1-85937-193-0	£8.99
England in the 1880s	1-85937-331-3	£17.99
English Castles (pb)	1-85937-434-4	£9.99
English Country Houses	1-85937-161-2	£17.99
Essex (pb)	1-85937-270-8	£9.99
Exeter	1-85937-126-4	£12.99
Exmoor	1-85937-132-9	£14.99
Falmouth	1-85937-066-7	£12.99
Folkestone (pb)	1-85937-124-8	£9.99
Glasgow (pb)	1-85937-190-6	£9.99
Gloucestershire	1-85937-102-7	£14.99
Great Yarmouth (pb)	1-85937-426-3	£9.99
Greater Manchester (pb)	1-85937-266-x	£9.99
Guildford (pb)	1-85937-410-7	£9.99
Hampshire (pb)	1-85937-279-1	£9.99
Hampshire Churches (pb)	1-85937-207-4	£9.99
Harrogate	1-85937-423-9	£9.99
Hastings & Bexhill (pb)	1-85937-131-0	£9.99
Heart of Lancashire (pb)	1-85937-197-3	£9.99
Helston (pb)	1-85937-214-7	£9.99
Hereford (pb)	1-85937-175-2	£9.99
Herefordshire	1-85937-174-4	£14.99
Hertfordshire (pb)	1-85937-247-3	£9.99
Horsham (pb)	1-85937-432-8	£9.99
Humberside	1-85937-215-5	£14.99
Hythe, Romney Marsh & Ashford	1-85937-256-2	£9.99

Available from your local bookshop or from the publisher

Frith Book Co Titles (continued)

Ipswich (pb)	1-85937-424-7	£9.99	St Ives (pb)	1-85937415-8	£9.99
Ireland (pb)	1-85937-181-7	£9.99	Scotland (pb)	1-85937-182-5	£9.99
Isle of Man (pb)	1-85937-268-6	£9.99	Scottish Castles (pb)	1-85937-323-2	£9.99
Isles of Scilly	1-85937-136-1	£14.99	Sevenoaks & Tunbridge	1-85937-057-8	£12.99
Isle of Wight (pb)	1-85937-429-8	£9.99	Sheffield, South Yorks (pb)	1-85937-267-8	£9.99
Isle of Wight Living Memories	1-85937-304-6	£14.99	Shrewsbury (pb)	1-85937-325-9	£9.99
Kent (pb)	1-85937-189-2	£9.99	Shropshire (pb)	1-85937-326-7	£9.99
Kent Living Memories	1-85937-125-6	£14.99	Somerset	1-85937-153-1	£14.99
Lake District (pb)	1-85937-275-9	£9.99	South Devon Coast	1-85937-107-8	£14.99
Lancaster, Morecambe & Heysham (pb)	1-85937-233-3	£9.99	South Devon Living Memories	1-85937-168-x	£14.99
Leeds (pb)	1-85937-202-3	£9.99	South Hams	1-85937-220-1	£14.99
Leicester	1-85937-073-x	£12.99	Southampton (pb)	1-85937-427-1	£9.99
Leicestershire (pb)	1-85937-185-x	£9.99	Southport (pb)	1-85937-425-5	£9.99
Lincolnshire (pb)	1-85937-433-6	£9.99	Staffordshire	1-85937-047-0	£12.99
Liverpool & Merseyside (pb)	1-85937-234-1	£9.99	Stratford upon Avon	1-85937-098-5	£12.99
London (pb)	1-85937-183-3	£9.99	Suffolk (pb)	1-85937-221-x	£9.99
Ludlow (pb)	1-85937-176-0	£9.99	Suffolk Coast	1-85937-259-7	£14.99
Luton (pb)	1-85937-235-x	£9.99	Surrey (pb)	1-85937-240-6	£9.99
Maidstone	1-85937-056-x	£14.99	Sussex (pb)	1-85937-184-1	£9.99
Manchester (pb)	1-85937-198-1	£9.99	Swansea (pb)	1-85937-167-1	£9.99
Middlesex	1-85937-158-2	£14.99	Tees Valley & Cleveland	1-85937-211-2	£14.99
New Forest	1-85937-128-0	£14.99	Thanet (pb)	1-85937-116-7	£9.99
Newark (pb)	1-85937-366-6	£9.99	Tiverton (pb)	1-85937-178-7	£9.99
Newport, Wales (pb)	1-85937-258-9	£9.99	Torbay	1-85937-063-2	£12.99
Newquay (pb)	1-85937-421-2	£9.99	Truro	1-85937-147-7	£12.99
Norfolk (pb)	1-85937-195-7	£9.99	Victorian and Edwardian Cornwall	1-85937-252-x	£14.99
Norfolk Living Memories	1-85937-217-1	£14.99	Victorian & Edwardian Devon	1-85937-253-8	£14.99
Northamptonshire	1-85937-150-7	£14.99	Victorian & Edwardian Kent	1-85937-149-3	£14.99
Northumberland Tyne & Wear (pb)	1-85937-281-3	£9.99	Vic & Ed Maritime Album	1-85937-144-2	£17.99
North Devon Coast	1-85937-146-9	£14.99	Victorian and Edwardian Sussex	1-85937-157-4	£14.99
North Devon Living Memories	1-85937-261-9	£14.99	Victorian & Edwardian Yorkshire	1-85937-154-x	£14.99
North London	1-85937-206-6	£14.99	Victorian Seaside	1-85937-159-0	£17.99
North Wales (pb)	1-85937-298-8	£9.99	Villages of Devon (pb)	1-85937-293-7	£9.99
North Yorkshire (pb)	1-85937-236-8	£9.99	Villages of Kent (pb)	1-85937-294-5	£9.99
Norwich (pb)	1-85937-194-9	£8.99	Villages of Sussex (pb)	1-85937-295-3	£9.99
Nottingham (pb)	1-85937-324-0	£9.99	Warwickshire (pb)	1-85937-203-1	£9.99
Nottinghamshire (pb)	1-85937-187-6	£9.99	Welsh Castles (pb)	1-85937-322-4	£9.99
Oxford (pb)	1-85937-411-5	£9.99	West Midlands (pb)	1-85937-289-9	£9.99
Oxfordshire (pb)	1-85937-430-1	£9.99	West Sussex	1-85937-148-5	£14.99
Peak District (pb)	1-85937-280-5	£9.99	West Yorkshire (pb)	1-85937-201-5	£9.99
Penzance	1-85937-069-1	£12.99	Weymouth (pb)	1-85937-209-0	£9.99
Peterborough (pb)	1-85937-219-8	£9.99	Wiltshire (pb)	1-85937-277-5	£9.99
Piers	1-85937-237-6	£17.99	Wiltshire Churches (pb)	1-85937-171-x	£9.99
Plymouth	1-85937-119-1	£12.99	Wiltshire Living Memories	1-85937-245-7	£14.99
Poole & Sandbanks (pb)	1-85937-251-1	£9.99	Winchester (pb)	1-85937-428-x	£9.99
Preston (pb)	1-85937-212-0	£9.99	Windmills & Watermills	1-85937-242-2	£17.99
Reading (pb)	1-85937-238-4	£9.99	Worcester (pb)	1-85937-165-5	£9.99
Romford (pb)	1-85937-319-4	£9.99	Worcestershire	1-85937-152-3	£14.99
Salisbury (pb)	1-85937-239-2	£9.99	York (pb)	1-85937-199-x	£9.99
Scarborough (pb)	1-85937-379-8	£9.99	Yorkshire (pb)	1-85937-186-8	£9.99
St Albans (pb)	1-85937-341-0	£9.99	Yorkshire Living Memories	1-85937-166-3	£14.99

See Frith books on the internet www.francisfrith.co.uk

FRITH PRODUCTS & SERVICES

Francis Frith would doubtless be pleased to know that the pioneering publishing venture he started in 1860 still continues today. A hundred and forty years later, The Francis Frith Collection continues in the same innovative tradition and is now one of the foremost publishers of vintage photographs in the world. Some of the current activities include:

Interior Decoration

Today Frith's photographs can be seen framed and as giant wall murals in thousands of pubs, restaurants, hotels, banks, retail stores and other public buildings throughout the country. In every case they enhance the unique local atmosphere of the places they depict and provide reminders of gentler days in an increasingly busy and frenetic world.

Product Promotions

Frith products are used by many major companies to promote the sales of their own products or to reinforce their own history and heritage. Frith promotions have been used by Hovis bread, Courage beers, Scots Porage Oats, Colman's mustard, Cadbury's foods, Mellow Birds coffee, Dunhill pipe tobacco, Guinness, and Bulmer's Cider.

Genealogy and Family History

As the interest in family history and roots grows world-wide, more and more people are turning to Frith's photographs of Great Britain for images of the towns, villages and streets where their ancestors lived; and, of course, photographs of the churches and chapels where their ancestors were christened, married and buried are an essential part of every genealogy tree and family album.

Frith Products

All Frith photographs are available Framed or just as Mounted Prints and Posters (size 23 x 16 inches). These may be ordered from the address below. From time to time other products - Address Books, Calendars, Table Mats, etc - are available.

The Internet

Already twenty thousand Frith photographs can be viewed and purchased on the internet through the Frith websites and a myriad of partner sites.

For more detailed information on Frith companies and products, look at these sites:

www.francisfrith.co.uk
www.francisfrith.com
(for North American visitors)

See the complete list of Frith Books at:

www.francisfrith.co.uk

This web site is regularly updated with the latest list of publications from the Frith Book Company. If you wish to buy books relating to another part of the country that your local bookshop does not stock, you may purchase on-line.

For further information, trade, or author enquiries please contact us at the address below:
The Francis Frith Collection, Frith's Barn, Teffont, Salisbury, Wiltshire, England SP3 5QP.
Tel: +44 (0)1722 716 376 Fax: +44 (0)1722 716 881   Email: sales@francisfrith.co.uk

See Frith books on the internet www.francisfrith.co.uk

TO RECEIVE YOUR FREE MOUNTED PRINT

Mounted Print
Overall size 14 x 11 inches

Cut out this Voucher and return it with your remittance for £1.95 to cover postage and handling, to UK addresses. For overseas addresses please include £4.00 post and handling. Choose any photograph included in this book. Your SEPIA print will be A4 in size, and mounted in a cream mount with burgundy rule line, overall size 14 x 11 inches.

Order additional Mounted Prints at HALF PRICE (only £7.49 each*)

If there are further pictures you would like to order, possibly as gifts for friends and family, purchase them at half price (no additional postage and handling required).

Have your Mounted Prints framed*

For an additional £14.95 per print you can have your chosen Mounted Print framed in an elegant polished wood and gilt moulding, overall size 16 x 13 inches (no additional postage and handling required).

---

* IMPORTANT!
These special prices are only available if ordered using the original voucher on this page (no copies permitted) and at the same time as your free Mounted Print, for delivery to the same address

---

Frith Collectors' Guild

From time to time we publish a magazine of news and stories about Frith photographs and further special offers of Frith products. If you would like 12 months FREE membership, please return this form.

Send completed forms to:
The Francis Frith Collection, Frith's Barn, Teffont, Salisbury, Wiltshire SP3 5QP

Voucher for FREE and Reduced Price Frith Prints

Picture no.	Page number	Qty	Mounted @ £7.49	Framed + £14.95	Total Cost
		1	**Free of charge***	£	£
			£7.49	£	£
			£7.49	£	£
			£7.49	£	£
			£7.49	£	£
			£7.49	£	£

Please allow 28 days for delivery   *** Post & handling** | **£1.95**

Book Title . . . .   **Total Order Cost** | **£**

Please do not photocopy this voucher. Only the original is valid, so please cut it out and return it to us.

I enclose a cheque / postal order for £ . . . .
made payable to 'The Francis Frith Collection'
OR please debit my Mastercard / Visa / Switch / Amex card
(credit cards please on all overseas orders)

Number . . . .

Issue No(Switch only) . . . . .Valid from (Amex/Switch) . . . .

Expires . . . .   Signature . . . .

Name Mr/Mrs/Ms . . . .

Address . . . .

. . . .

. . . .

. . . . Postcode . . . .

Daytime Tel No . . . .   Valid to 31/12/03

The Francis Frith Collectors' Guild

Please enrol me as a member for 12 months free of charge.

Name Mr/Mrs/Ms . . . .

Address . . . .

. . . .

. . . . Postcode . . . .

Would you like to find out more about Francis Frith?

We have recently recruited some entertaining speakers who are happy to visit local groups, clubs and societies to give an illustrated talk documenting Frith's travels and photographs. If you are a member of such a group and are interested in hosting a presentation, we would love to hear from you.

Our speakers bring with them a small selection of our local town and county books, together with sample prints. They are happy to take orders. A small proportion of the order value is donated to the group who have hosted the presentation. The talks are therefore an excellent way of fundraising for small groups and societies.

Can you help us with information about any of the Frith photographs in this book?

We are gradually compiling an historical record for each of the photographs in the Frith archive. It is always fascinating to find out the names of the people shown in the pictures, as well as insights into the shops, buildings and other features depicted.

If you recognize anyone in the photographs in this book, or if you have information not already included in the author's caption, do let us know. We would love to hear from you, and will try to publish it in future books or articles.

Our production team

Frith books are produced by a small dedicated team at offices in the converted Grade II listed 18th-century barn at Teffont near Salisbury, illustrated above. Most have worked with the Frith Collection for many years. All have in common one quality: they have a passion for the Frith Collection. The team is constantly expanding, but currently includes:

Jason Buck, John Buck, Douglas Burns, Heather Crisp, Lucy Elcock, Isobel Hall, Rob Hames, Hazel Heaton, Peter Horne, James Kinnear, Tina Leary, Hannah Marsh, Eliza Sackett, Terence Sackett, Sandra Sanger, Lewis Taylor, Shelley Tolcher, Helen Vimpany, Clive Wathen and Jenny Wathen.